SEELEY-SWAN DAY HIKES

INTRODUCTION

What is a day hike? For the purposes of this guide a day hike ranges from one mile to 16 miles, round trip.

This trail guide includes day hikes in the 73,877-acre Mission Mountains Wilderness (the east-facing slope of the Mission Mountains Range), maintained by the USDA Forest Service. Elevations range from 4,500 feet to 9,300 feet. This guide does not include trails in the Mission Mountains Tribal Wilderness (the west-facing slope of the Mission Mountains). There are approximately 45 miles of maintained Forest Service trails in the Mission Mountains Wilderness. Most trails are best suited to hiking rather than horseback riding due to the rugged terrain and because they are relatively short. Throughout the Mission Mountain Wilderness, you will encounter abandoned Indian and packer trails. These are difficult to follow and are suitable only for the most experienced hikers with map and compass skills.

The Mission Mountains Wilderness was so designated on January 4, 1975. The laws that govern its use are outlined in the Congressional Wilderness Act of 1964. As such, mountain bikes, hang gliders, motorized trail bikes, motorcycles, four-wheel drive vehicles, and snowmobiles are not permitted.

This guide also includes the Swan Front Range. Although the valley facing western slope of the Swan Front Range does not include the Bob Marshall Wilderness, some of the trails described in this guide were constructed for the purpose of providing access into the "Bob." Other trails described in this guide were developed to lead hikers to outstanding features along the Front Range. The Bob Marshall Wilderness is a 1,009,356-acre wildland area on the Flathead and Lewis and Clark National Forests. One fourth larger than Rhode Island, the Bob was established as a wilderness area by Congress the first year the Wilderness Act was instituted in 1964.

I have elected to exclude several hiking destinations from this guide. Descriptions to places like Fatty Lake, Cat Lake, Pony Lake, Upper Rumble Lake, the Jim Lakes Basin, and Gray Wolf Lake are not listed. Access to these involves crossing private land, reservation land, or traveling on unmaintained paths.

ABOUT THE AUTHOR

Alan Leftridge has been a wilderness ranger in the Mission Mountains Wilderness Area and a seasonal naturalist in Yellowstone National Park. He earned a B.S. degree in biology at Central Missouri State University, a Ph.D. in science education at Kansas State University, and a teaching credential from the University of Montana. Since 1973, he has taught high school science in West Yellowstone, science courses at Miami University, in Ohio, and environmental studies at Humboldt State University, California. He is the executive editor of The Interpreter magazine of the National Association for Interpretation, and has authored Interpretive Writing, InterpPress, Glacier Day Hikes, and Going to Glacier, Farcountry Press.
Alan lives in the Swan Valley.

Copyright © 2008, Alan Leftridge.
Post Office Box 976
Swan Valley, Montana 59826
leftridge@blackfoot.net, leftridge.com

Design: LK Duvanich
Cover photograph: Upper Cold Lake
Title page photograph: Glacier Lake Trail

All of the photographs in this guide are by the author
Printed in China by Global Interprint, Inc., Santa Rosa, California

CONTENTS

The Valley Floor

The Swan Front

Nature Trails

TRAIL TIPS

There are a few considerations that will enhance your hiking experiences in the Seeley-Swan:

Many of the access roads and trails are not passable until June.

Plan ahead. Visit one of the USDA Forest Service ranger stations in Seeley Lake or Big Fork, or the Swan Ecosytem Center in Condon to inquire about conditions.

Check the trailhead for ranger-posted alerts.

Walk single file to stop the erosion caused by trail widening.

Travel on established, durable, designated trails. Short cuts can be dangerous and lead to erosion.

Leave no trace. Leave what you find, unless it is something that someone else has carelessly misplaced. Yield to uphill hikers when the trail is a single path.

Give-way to stock users. Stand on the downhill side and away from the trail.

Bicycles are permitted on designated trails.

Respect the needs of wildlife. Allow wildlife to step off the trail before approaching.

Never approach a bear.

Leave the area and plan to complete your hike another day if a grizzly bear is in the area.

HIKE DESIGNATIONS

EASY

Crystal Lake
Glacier Lake
Morrell Falls
Clearwater Lake
Everchanging Forest
East Foothills Trail
Glacier Slough
Holland Falls
Holland Lake Nature Trail

Clearwater Game Range
Swan River Nature Trail
Goat Creek Watchable Wildlife Trail
Big Larch Nature Trail
Sprunger-Whitney Nature Trail
Clearwater River Canoe Trail
Jim Girard Memorial Tamaracks Grove
Swan River National Wildlife Refuge
Sally Tollefson Trail

MODERATE

Cedar Lake
Cold Lakes
Crescent Lake and Heart Lake
Hemlock Lake
East Holland Lake Connector
Lake Dinah
The Jewel Basin
Inspiration Point
Bond Lake
Elbow Lookout

STRENUOUS

Piper Lake
Turquoise Lake
Pyramid Pass
Smith Creek Pass
Sapphire Lake and Upper Holland Lake
Sixmile Peak
Hall Lake

CONSIDERATIONS

Both black bears and grizzly bears live within the Mission Mountains Wilderness, on the Seeley-Swan Valley Floor, and along the Swan Front Range. Avoid a confrontation with a bear by taking a few precautions:

> • *Hike with companions during the mid-morning to mid-afternoon. These are the hours that bears are less active.*
>
> • *Make your presence known, particularly near blind turns, densely forested areas, and in windy conditions.*
>
> • *Inquire at a ranger station or the Swan Ecosystem Center to learn if bears have been sighted in the area you will explore.*
>
> • *Stay at least 100 feet from a bear.*

Mountain lions are common yet elusive. The chances of seeing a lion on your walk are remote, as they usually withdraw from sight when they detect humans. There has not been a reported attack on a human by a lion within the range of this guide.

Mosquitoes abound in the Seeley-Swan area during the warm months. Swarms of mosquitoes are encountered in cool, damp areas as well as warm, sunny hillsides. Mosquitoes are attracted to carbon dioxide. They can easily detect the gas and the warm, moist air around you. Protect yourself by using insect repellents that contain citronella or 28-30% DEET, and by wearing protective clothing. Long sleeves, pants, and socks, as well as a bandana tied around your neck that has been sprayed with a repellent are most effective for keeping mosquitoes from biting.

Weather extremes are possible. Lightning and thunderstorms occur with little notice in the high country. It can snow any month.

Drinking-water sources are not available at any of the trailheads. Bring ample water for your hike. Your body will require more water than normal when hiking during summer days, on strenuous hikes, and along south and western-facing exposed trails.

HOW TO USE THIS BOOK

Travel rating
Descriptions of Easy, Moderate, and Strenuous are based on terrain and trail condition, not the length of the trail. Easy walks will have little elevation gain and will be on well maintained, soft surfaced trails. Strenuous walks will have terrain diversity and are often over broken, loose rock surfaces. An easy trail may be lengthy and accomplished by anyone, with ample time. A strenuous trail may be short but demanding, even for experienced hikers.

Distance and Elevation Change
Distances and elevation changes are from published USDA Forest Service data.

Trail Use
Trail usage has been categorized as either light, moderate, or heavy. These terms are arbitrary, based upon my experiences walking the trails of the Seeley-Swan. The category descriptions are as follows. Light: expect up to six visitors over the duration of your hike. Moderate: seven to fifteen visitors on the trail. Heavy: more than fifteen visitors on the trail.

Walking time
Two miles is the distance an average adult would be expected to cover in an hour, even with frequent stops to discover and experience the wonders of the surroundings.

Getting there
Montana State Highway 83 is the only paved road passing through the Seeley-Swan Valley. The highway begins at the junction of Montana Highway 200 and terminates at Montana Highway 35, north of Big Fork. All of the side roads identified in this guide are located by the mile markers along Highway 83. The mile markers begin at the junction of Highways 200 and 83.

Along the way
I have chosen to provide information about the trails as distances from the trailhead rather than provide maps that are not to scale.

CEDAR LAKE

Travel rating: Moderate.
Distance: 7.2 miles, round trip.
Walking time: 3 to 4 hours, round trip.
Trail use: Light. Hiking and horseback riding.
Elevation change: 1,485 feet gain to Saddle, 300 feet drop to lake.

Getting there
Turn on to Fatty Creek Road, between mile markers 58 and 59, Highway 83. The road to the Cedar Lake trailhead is 10 rugged miles. Low-clearance vehicles can navigate the road, but the going can be slow. The parking area can accommodate 15 vehicles.

Along the way
0.1 miles. Enter the Mission Mountains Wilderness.
0.5 miles. First switchback.
2.0 miles. No Name Lake.
2.3 miles. Begin ascent to saddle.
3.0 miles. Saddle. 7,592 feet Cedar Point is to your left.
3.6 miles. Cedar Lake.

The Cedar Lake drainage flows east-southeast. The creek that you are following, and the drainage you are in, is Fatty Creek. The waters you hear are coming from the Rainbow Lake and the No Name Lake area. You will enter the Cedar Lake drainage after passing over the saddle at the three-mile mark. At the saddle you will see Cedar Point to your immediate left. You will soon get your first view of Cedar Lake in a basin. At 456 acres, Cedar Lake is in one of the most beautiful settings in the Mission Mountains. The lake is surrounded by peaks, giving the feeling of being deep in wild country. Cedar Lake is near the northern boundary of the 73,877-acre Mission Mountains Wilderness.
There are very few cedar trees around the lake or on the trail. You will encounter more Western red cedar trees along the road to the trailhead than you will see during your walk. At 6,520 feet in elevation, Cedar Lake is at the upper elevation limit of the Western red cedar. The name of the lake comes from the Cedar Creek drainage with its numerous cedar trees.

The trail begins as a gentle climb through a mature larch/fir forest. The switchbacks on the first two miles of the trail are easy to walk, and the footing is good. Look for old USDA Forest Service blaze marks on the trees. The blaze marks are about eight feet off the ground and are a four-inch square on top of a four by eight inch rectangle cut into the bark of the trees. The USDA Forest Service used the blazes to mark the trail before the Mission Mountains Wilderness was designated on January 4, 1975. After walking for two miles, you will come to a small lake. The lake is referred to as No Name Lake. Most hikers have Cedar Lake or beyond as their destination; therefore, No Name Lake is seldom used or explored.

After leaving No Name Lake, you will encounter a slough half the size of No Name Lake. This slough was once a lake along the Rainbow Lake drainage. The lake filled with sediment. This slough will someday be forested. After leaving the slough, you begin a climb over the saddle and into the Cedar Lake basin. The switchbacks along this one-mile stretch of trail are moderately strenuous.

Expect to find snow on the upper portions of the trail until early July. As the snow recedes, glacier lilies flourish near the trail. Mid-July to mid-August will bring a profusion of alpine wildflowers to areas recently covered by snow. You will discover large gardens of beargrass, asters, monkeyflowers, and paintbrush.

COLD LAKES

Travel rating: Moderate.
Distance: 3.6 miles, round trip.
Walking time: 2 hours, round trip.
Trail use: Moderate. Hiking.
Elevation change: 425 feet gain to Lower, 978 feet gain to Upper.

There are two Cold Lakes, Upper and Lower. They are about the same acreage. The walk to the first, Lower Cold Lake, takes you through a mature spruce/fir forest. Listen for the song of the winter wren. They sing a fast-paced sweet, melodic song.
Notice the wide spacing of the trees. Adequate sunlight and moisture allow prodigious undergrowth of beargrass and Devil's club. This lush understory nearly obscures the trail in several areas. The undergrowth has not been removed from encroaching on the trail due to the difficulty of such a project. It would need to be accomplished by hand since legislative decree has forbidden the use of power tools in designated wilderness areas. This is bear and moose habitat. The likelihood of encountering either is low. Yet the thick undergrowth restricts visibility and heightens the anxiety of the possibility of startling a big mammal along your walk. Make your presence known, and revel in the fact that you are experiencing very wild country.

Getting there

Turn on to Cold Lake Road, between mile markers 46 and 47, Highway 83. The road to Cold Lake trailhead is well marked and seven miles. The first five miles is well maintained. The last two miles to the trailhead is rough, yet passable for any vehicle. The parking area at the trailhead can accommodate 15 vehicles.

Along the way

0.3 miles. Enter the Mission Mountains Wilderness.

0.5 miles. Cross a seasonal creek. Look for a seasonal 20- foot waterfall to the right of the trail. This drains the meadow you arrive at before reaching Lower Cold Lake.

0.6 miles. Cross the North Fork of Cold Creek.

0.7 miles. Small stream flows under a standing Douglas-fir.

1.0 miles. Cross the North Fork of Cold Creek on a large log. The North Fork is 3.5 miles long from Cold Lake to Cold Creek.

1.5 miles. Meadow from which the seasonal creek originates. Look for a large spruce tree along the trail that was killed by lightning in July 1997. Notice the spiral effect of the bark missing from the trunk. Look for the effects a 1999 fire across the meadow.

1.8 miles. Cold Lake.

The Lower Cold Lake area is heavily forested with rugged mountain terrain on three sides. At 80 acres, Lower Cold is deep and well within the Mission Mountains Wilderness. Upon reaching the lake, you will be attracted to the sound of rushing water at the far end. Lower Cold Lake is fed by a cascading stream from Upper Cold Lake, sometimes called Frigid Lake. The lakes are almost identical in size, only 0.25 miles apart.

There is no camping within 0.25 miles of either lake. A maintained trail to Upper Cold Lake is not kept. Except for having to climb over and crawl under significant mature forest downfall, the access to Upper Cold Lake is easy. Extending your hike to Upper Cold Lake will add an additional 30 minutes to your adventure. Nonetheless, you will be rewarded with experiencing two very lovely western Montana alpine lakes.

CRESCENT LAKE AND HEART LAKE

Travel rating: Moderate.
Distance: 8.0 miles, round trip.
Walking time: 4 hours, round trip.
Trail use: Moderate. Hiking.
Elevation change: 1,220 feet gain to Crescent Lake,
*   1,329 feet gain to Heart Lake.*

Getting there

The trail is easily accessible by way of a USDA Forest Service road. Turn on to Kraft Creek Road between mile markers 37 and 38, Highway 83. Follow the gravel road 11 miles to the trailhead. The road is kept in good condition. The parking area is large and can accommodate 20 vehicles. Most of the cars in the parking lot will belong to people who will not have Crescent Lake or Heart Lake as their destination.

The trailhead serves as an embarkation point for day hikes to Glacier Lake, Lace Lake, Turquoise Lake, and numerous overnight locations deep in the Mission Mountains Wilderness.

Heart Lake and the Post Creek Saddle

14

Along the way
0.4 miles. Cross Crazy Horse Creek.
0.7 miles. Cross Crescent Creek.
1.2 miles. Trail junction to Glacier Lake.
2.7 miles. Trail junction to Turquoise Lake.
3.5 miles. Crescent Lake.
4.0 miles. Heart Lake.

The trail begins by winding through old-growth Englemann spruce and Douglas-fir. The distance between the trees allows an open forest floor and a wide diversity of plant and animal life. After leaving the trail junction to Glacier Lake, the forest is dominated by old-growth larch and Douglas-fir. At this point the trail becomes a series of long switchbacks through the open forest. The grade of the trail makes for easy walking. Expect to encounter mosquitos along the trail.

At 2.7 miles you will arrive at the Turquoise Lake/Crescent Lake trail junction. The final 0.75 miles to Crescent Lake is on a maintained but brushy trail. The walk from the junction is moderate. At an elevation above 6,000 feet, Crescent Lake is 24 acres and 35 feet deep, offering beautiful reflections of the surrounding mountains.

If you choose to continue to Heart Lake, you will find it another 0.5 miles from the eastern shore of Crescent Lake. Follow the unmaintained but well-worn trail around the south shore of Crescent Lake and up the hill to the west of the lake. Heart Lake is at a higher elevation than Crescent Lake. It is 13 acres and approximately 55 feet deep. Heart Lake has some beautiful rock outcroppings near its southern shore. A small island is accessible if you are willing to wade to your waist.

Island Lake is farther to the west in the chain of lakes with yet an unnamed lake above it. Access to Island Lake is difficult and tricky. A trail is not available. A map and compass or personal guide is needed in order to find the lake.

As you look to the west of Heart Lake, you will notice a saddle (pass) through the mountain range. This is the Post Creek Saddle. The saddle is at the headwaters that feeds this chain of lakes.

CRYSTAL LAKE

Travel rating: Easy to Moderate.
Distance: 4.4 miles, round trip.
Walking time: 6 hours, round trip.
Use: Moderate. Hiking.
Elevation change: 945 feet loss.

The Crystal Lake Trail provides an easy hike downhill to a large alpine lake. The trail is on the south-facing side of Crystal Creek drainage. The walk to and from Crystal Lake is a steady descent and ascent. The trail is open to the forest canopy in several places. The walk down to Crystal Lake can be easy any time of the day. The hike back up to the trailhead is more difficult, especially if attempted after noon. It is advised that you begin your hike back to the trailhead before the afternoon sun and that you take plenty of water.

Crystal Lake is 186 acres and at an elevation of 4,755 feet. Drainages feeding Crystal Lake come from Lost Lake and High Park Lake. After leaving Crystal Lake, the creek flows about one mile before entering the Swan River. Crystal Lake has several undeveloped campsites along its shores. This is a favorite destination for people wanting to make an easy overnight backpacking trip and use the campsite as a staging area for day hikes deep into the Mission Mountains Wilderness.

Getting there

Take Highway 83 to Lindbergh Lake Road, USDA Forest Service Road Number 79, between mile markers 34 and 35. The road to the Crystal Lake trailhead is well maintained and passable throughout the warmer seasons. At two miles veer to the right toward the Lindbergh Lake Campground. Another one mile will have you turn off the main road toward Bunyan Lake (still USDA Forest Service Road Number 79). Follow the road an additional nine miles to the trailhead. There is space for six vehicles in the parking lot.

Along the way
0.2 miles. Cross a clearcut. Meadow Lake is to your right.
0.3 miles. Begin descent into the Crystal Lake drainage.
0.7 miles. Enter the Mission Mountains Wilderness.
1.5 miles. Cross the first of several streams.
2.1 miles. Trail junction. Trail signs point to Crystal Lake,
BeaverCreek, and Meadow Lake.
2.2 miles. Crystal Lake.

The Crystal Lake Trail has plenty of natural history features to
interest any hiker. Bears, grouses, and deer make this area their
home. The forest is a diverse mix of Douglas-firs, Western larch
trees, Pacific yews, and the Montana state tree, ponderosa pine.
You will encounter several large ponderosa pines along your
hike. These trees reach diameters of six or more feet and are often
referred to as yellowbellies. Other popular names for ponderosa
pines are yellow pine, p-pine, and bull pine. Take the
opportunity to smell the trunk of one of the trees along the trail.
The tree might be giving off a fragrance if it is a particularly
warm day. What fragrance do you detect? A good resource for
the natural history of the ponderosa pine is, *Graced by Pines:
The Ponderosa Pine in the American West*, by Alexandra Murphy.
The book is available at the Swan Ecosystem Center, mile marker
42, Highway 83.

Crystal Lake, near the outlet

GLACIER LAKE

Travel rating: Easy.
Distance: 3.2 miles, round trip.
Walking time: 2 hours, round trip.
Trail use: Heavy. Hiking and horseback riding.
Elevation change: 425 feet gain.

The trail to Glacier Lake is a premier hike in the Mission Mountains Range. Is is an easy walk that can be accomplished by most family members. The trail provides some of the best scenery in the Mission Mountains. It is long enough to make you feel that you have been on a wilderness hike but short enough to not be too tiring.

The trail and lake are on the east slope of the Mission Mountains Range. Consequently, the trail can be snow-covered and the lake icy until mid-June. The trail can be wet until July, even when free of snow.

Getting there
The trail is easily accessible by way of a USDA Forest Service road. Turn onto Kraft Creek Road, mile marker 37, Highway 83. Follow the gravel road 11 miles to the trailhead. The road is kept in good condition. The parking area is large and can accommodate 20 vehicles. Drinking water is not available; a pit toilet is located near the parking area. The parking lot may have several cars, but not all of the visitors will have Glacier Lake as their destination. The Glacier Lake Trail comprises the lower section of trails that lead to Crescent Lake, Heart Lake, Island Lake, and Turquoise Lake.

Along the way
0.6 miles. Cross Crazy Horse Creek.
0.8 miles. Enter the Mission Mountains Wilderness.
0.9 miles. Cross Crescent Creek. Half-way to Glacier Lake.
1.2 miles. Rock outcropping.
1.3 miles. Crescent, Heart, Island, and Turquoise Lake Trail.
1.6 miles. Glacier Lake.

I consider the trail to Glacier Lake to be the most diverse and lovely day hike in the Swan Valley. The trail begins on part of an abandoned access road and narrows to a beautiful undulating pathway. The view of the trail and the distant Mission Mountains range during the first 0.25 miles is picturesque. The walking experience is all the more delightful with the sounds and sights of Glacier Creek to the south. You will likely be serenaded along the way by the varied thrush.

The trail winds through old-growth Englemann's spruce and Douglas-fir. Notice the distance between the huge trees and the openness of the forest floor.

The open forest floor allows for a wide diversity of plant and animal life due to the availability of sunlight.

Most hikers will consider Glacier Lake their final destination. Glacier Lake is a 104, acre snow-fed lake at 5,260 feet.

Note the restoration efforts made by wilderness rangers around the shore of the lake. Respect for the restoration efforts will assure that Glacier Lake will retain its wild character. The area is managed for day use only. No camping.

If you start your walk early in the morning, you may arrive at Glacier Lake without seeing another hiker. Along the trail and at Glacier Lake, you might see osprey, bald eagles, Columbian ground squirrels, whitetailed-deer, and bears. You might encounter 20 or 30 hikers on your return to the parking lot. Nonetheless, you will have experienced the solitude of hiking on a truly wonderful trail, and the serenity of being alone at one of the most beautiful lake settings in Montana.

HEMLOCK LAKE

> Travel rating: Moderate.
> Distance: 6.4 miles, round trip.
> Walking time: 4 hours, round trip.
> Trail use: Light. Hiking, horseback riding.
> Elevation change: 870 feet gain.

On August 10, 2003, A lightning-caused fire started in the Crazy Horse Drainage south of Hemlock Lake. The fire burned most of the Hemlock Lake area. Exploring this area on a regular basis will allow you to measure how a forest recovers from fire.

Getting there.
Turn onto Kraft Creek Road between mile markers 37 and 38, Highway 83. Follow the gravel road seven miles to the Hemlock Trail #607 sign. Follow this access road one mile to the trailhead. The parking area can accommodate 10 vehicles. Hemlock Lake is a high alpine lake that receives little visitation. It is at an elevation of 6,220 feet and is 30 acres.

The first 1.3 miles of the trail climbs through a logged area. It receives direct sunlight throughout the day. Temperatures can be hot along the trail by late morning. The creek you hear to your left is Red Butte. You do not cross Red Butte during your walk, but will be listening to its rushing waters for the first 1.5 miles.

At 1.3 miles you enter the Mission Mountains Wilderness where the trail traverses its way into the Hemlock Creek drainage. Here you will be walking through areas burned with high intensity and other areas of low intensity. There also will be "islands" of forest not burned. This patterning makes up a "burn mosaic."

Before the fire the forest was mountain hemlocks, spruce trees, Pacific yews, Douglas-firs, beargrasses, and huckleberries. Today it is an explosion of pioneer wildflowers. The last 0.25 miles of the trail to Hemlock Lake is a steep uphill grade. This section of the trail begins within 40 paces after you cross Hemlock Creek (the second major creek you encounter). The trail is open to sunlight, bring ample drinking water. Expect mosquitoes at the lake.

ELBOW LOOKOUT

Travel rating: Easy.
Distance: 2.5 miles, round trip. Light.
Walking time: 2 hours, round trip.
Trail use: Hiking, horseback riding.
Elevation change: 890 feet gain.

Getting there.
Turn on to Lindbergh Lake Road (USDA Forest Service Road 79) between mile markers 34 and 35, Highway 83. Travel three miles and follow the road to the Lindbergh Lake Campground. An international-style hiker sign is located to the right of the road before you enter the campground. There is ample parking nearby.

The Elbow Lookout Trail is a short walk from the campground to an abandoned USDA Forest Service lookout tower site. The tower was removed long ago, although concrete footings remain. The site overlooks the upper Swan Valley and the length of Lindbergh Lake. Views must have been spectacular from the tower. The trail traverses the mountainside north of Lindbergh Lake. The dominant forest plants include Douglas fir, Western larch, mountain maple, Oregon grape, and beargrass. The trail is narrow and straight with soft footing.

The trail was constructed to serve as a supply-line for rangers at the tower. Look for telephone wires still attached to some of the older trees along the trail. At 0.3 miles, the trail affords great views of the elbow bend area of Lindbergh Lake. The views are possible because the forest is now mixed with old growth ponderosa pine trees. At 0.5 miles, the trail enters a clear-cut. Most of the smaller trees in this area are lodgepole pines.

You will not see the foot of the Lindbergh Lake from the lookout area. Look for the foot of the lake from the openings along the trail. From these you will see the terminal moraine rubble that serves as a dam for the lake. At the lookout you will see the low-lying glacial deposit hills, made by the Swan Valley glacier, that form the southern extent of the Swan River Valley drainage. On the other side of these hills is the Clearwater River drainage.

PIPER LAKE

Travel rating: Strenuous.
Distance: 9.6 miles, round trip.
Walking time: 6 hours, round trip.
Trail use: Light. Hiking and horseback riding.
Elevation change: 2,090 feet gain.

Piper Lake is 83 acres. At an elevation of 6,293 feet, the lake is in a remarkably picturesque setting. It is surrounded by a diverse forest, rocky cliff faces, and mountain peaks. From the north shore of the lake, you will experience a good view of the Swan Range to the east and the Ducharme Lake/Piper Crow Pass area to the southwest. The forest is mixed, with subalpine firs, spruce trees, and white pines. Pikas inhabit the rock faces. Bears and moose also live in the area.

Most trail guides that include Piper Lake suggest you access Piper Lake by way of Cedar Lake Trail and the connector trail from Cedar Lake. This involves a 16-mile round-trip hike through rugged country. Many people who hike to Piper Lake do it as an overnight backpacking trip. I have chosen to offer the Piper Lake trail as a day hike that is appropriate for the well-conditioned backcountry hiker. Whether you choose to access Piper Lake from Cedar Lake via the connecting trail or the Piper Lake trail, you will be treated to a beautiful subalpine lake environment.

Getting there
Turn onto Piper Creek Road, between mile markers 53 and 54, Highway 83. The road to Piper Lake trailhead is a well-marked five-mile long road. The parking area at the trailhead can accommodate seven vehicles. Take care not to block one of the road barricades.

Along the way
0.3 miles. Cross Piper Creek.
0.5 miles. Leave logged area.
1.6 miles. Enter the Mission Mountains Wilderness Area.
2.8 miles. Seasonal potholes.
3.4 miles. Trail junction to Piper/Crow Pass.
4.8 miles. Piper Lake.

The length of Piper Lake Trail has three features: an easy walk, a challenging hike, and a rigorous climb. The trail skirts a logging operation and creek corridor for the first 0.25 miles. The forest is made up predominantly of Western red cedar trees with corresponding riparian habitat. It is here that visitors can find refuge from a hot summer day. The creek offers several places for the casual walker to find a peaceful pool and abundant bird life.

The next three miles of Piper Lake Trail is moderate in difficulty. This section of the trail follows Piper Creek. The trail itself is undulating, with short sections of ascent followed by rapid descent. The trail is similar to the design of a children's roller-coaster ride. Nonetheless, even with the roller-coaster effect, the trail continues an ascent toward the lake.

The last section of the trail is a steep uphill climb of one mile. The trail switches back and traverses several rock outcroppings. This upper section of the trail offers a striking contrast to the forest floor.

Rock outcroppings with a profusion of seasonal wildflowers abound. You will also be treated to some great views of the interior of the Mission Mountains Wilderness Area. All aspects of the trail considered, it is rated as strenuous for a hiker seeking Piper Lake as his or her destination.

TURQUOISE LAKE

Travel rating:
Strenuous.

Distance:
11 miles, round trip.

Walking time:
6 hours, round trip.

Trail use:
Moderate. Hiking.

Elevation change:
1,589 feet gain.

Turquoise Lake is a deep
184-acre alpine lake
nestled beneath Glacier
Peaks, Sunset Glacier, Lone Pine Pass, and Panoramic Peak. The
trail is rated as a strenuous hike in part due to the fact that the
trail is ill defined beyond Lagoon Lake. A map and compass, or
guide is recommended to help you find Turquoise Lake.

Getting there
The trail is easily accessible by way of a USDA Forest Service road.
Turn on to Kraft Creek Road between mile markers 37 and 38,
Highway 83. Follow the gravel road 11 miles to the trailhead.
The road is kept in good condition. The parking area is large
and can accommodate 20 vehicles. Most of the people whose
cars are in the parking lot will not have Turquoise Lake as their
destination. The trailhead serves as a embarkation point for day
hikes to Glacier Lake, Crescent Lake, Heart Lake, and numerous
overnight locations deep in the Mission Mountains Wilderness.
Consequently, you may encounter day-use hikers, fishermen, and
overnight backpackers heading to different destinations.

Along the way
0.4 miles. Cross Crazy Horse Creek.
0.7 miles. Cross Crescent Creek.
1.2 miles. Trail junction to Glacier Lake.
2.7 miles. Trail junction to Crescent Lake and Heart Lake.
4.0 miles. Panoramic view of Swan Range, Glacier Lake,
Lindy Peak, and Daughter of the Sun Mountain.
5.1 miles. Lagoon Lake.
5.5 miles. Turquoise Lake.

*The trail begins by winding among old-growth Englemann's
spruces and Douglas-firs. The distance between the trees allows
an open forest floor and a diversity of plant and animal life. After
leaving the trail junction to Glacier Lake, the forest is dominated
by old-growth larch and Douglas-fir trees. Here, the trail becomes
a series of long switchbacks through the open forest. The grade of
the trail is easy to manage. Listen for the call of the varied thrush.
The call is a high-pitched ringing sound. The trail maintains a
steady climb through the forest until the four-mile mark. At this
point you break out onto an open mountainside, and you will
have magnificent views of Glacier Lake directly below, Lindy Peak
to the immediate south, the Swan Range to the east, and the
Turquoise Lake area ahead of you and to your left. Listen for the
bugle of pikas (rock rabbits) in this area.*

*The trail is poorly defined beyond Lagoon Lake, because it
traverses slab rock and is difficult to detect. Soon after leaving
Lagoon Lake you will see Lace Lake below you and to your left.
Do not walk down to Lace Lake if your destination is Turquoise
Lake. Stay well above Lace Lake and keep it to your left. After
Lagoon Lake, you will encounter two substantial streams. The
second is the outlet of Turquoise Lake. Follow the stream up.
Turquoise Lake is in a high, wild alpine setting.*

*Be mindful of rapidly changing weather conditions. Weather can
turn violent with little forwarning. Look for mountain goats on
the rock faces and bald eagles soaring over the lake. Listen to the
rushing waters from snow and the silence of the wilderness.*

EAST FOOTHILLS

Travel rating: Easy.
Distance: 12 miles, round trip.
Walking time: 6 hours, round trip.
Trail use: Light. Hiking and horseback riding.
Elevation change: 140 feet loss.

The East Foothills Trail offers a quiet, leisurely experience. The walk will give you an introduction to the environment of the lower Swan Front and the Seeley-Swan Valley floor. It is the only remaining section of a trail that once traversed the Swan Range from The Summit (mile marker 32) to Swan Lake. The trail can be accessed from the Holland Lake area via Trail 415 or the Cooney Lookout. Most trail users travel from the north to the south, relying on a source of transportation at Holland Lake to return them to the trailhead near the Cooney Lookout. Concluding your walk at Holland Lake will allow you to visit the historic Holland Lake Lodge, where you can enjoy a refreshment, a meal, or a swim at the Forest Service-maintained public beach.

Getting there
The trail is easily accessible by way of a good road. Turn on to Rumble Creek Road, mile marker 40, Highway 83. The gravel road is maintained by Missoula County the first three miles. The last mile is maintained by the Forest Service and is passable for all vehicles. Follow the road to the Cooney Lookout tower. Continue around the tower another 0.25 miles to the trailhead. There is parking for six vehicles.

White-tailed Deer
This is the most common deer you will see in the Seeley-Swan Valley. They can live to be 16 years old in the wild.

Vehicles, predators, and hunters are the main reasons that individuals rarely live that long in the valley.

Along the way
0.2 miles. The trail begins to traverse the Swan Front.
0.3 miles. Pass below a burn area.
0.4 miles. Cross Rumble Creek on a footbridge.
0.5 miles. Unmarked "man-way" to Rumble Lake.
0.8 miles. Cross the South Fork of Rumble Creek. Look for a series
of waterfalls upstream from the footbridge.
0.9 miles. Pass below a burn area.
1.5 miles. Cross Buck Creek on a footbridge.
2.2 miles. Trail drops on to an old logging road.
3.5 miles. Enter a mature Western larch/Pacific yew forest.
3.7 miles. Cross Barber Creek on a footbridge.
4.0 miles. Trail drops on to an old logging road.
4.4 miles. Trail crosses a new logging road. Glimpse Holland Lake
to your right and enter the Holland Creek drainage.
4.7 miles. Trail junction. USDA Forest Service Trail #415.
6.0 miles. Trailhead.

The trail is mostly level except near the streams. You will cross
four significant creeks and several seasonal water courses.
Footbridges have been constructed over the four creeks. You may
expect to get your feet wet crossing the seasonal streams.
Nonetheless, the forest itself is relatively dry compared to the
east-facing Mission Mountains front. It is likely that you will be
the only hiker on the trail until you reach USDA Forest Service
Trail #415. At this point you will be sharing the trail with
hikers and stock users going to and coming from the Bob
Marshall Wilderness.

During your walk you will encounter mature larch trees, Pacific
yews, and lodgepole pine trees, lightning-caused burn areas,
prescribed burn areas, and old logged parcels. The forest is open,
except near the drainages. The seasonal drainages have dense
undergrowth that crowd the trail. The Swan Front supports
populations of whitetailed-deer, mule deer, elk, mountain lions,
bobcats, fishers, black bears, and grizzly bears. This is a good trail
to look for and listen to the Townsend's warbler.

EAST HOLLAND LAKE CONNECTOR

Travel rating: Easy to Moderate.
Distance: 6.3 mile loop.
Walking time: 4 hours.
Trail use: Moderate. Hiking and horseback riding.
Elevation change: 892 feet gain.

Many day hikers will walk the first two miles to Holland Creek, have lunch, and return the same way. Other hikers may wish to continue beyond Holland Creek on the Holland-Gordon Trail and make a loop around Holland Lake. It is the last 0.5 miles before reaching Holland Creek that the trail offers the most outstanding panoramic views of Holland Lake and the Mission Mountains.

Like most trails along the Swan Front, it is advised to start your walk in the morning during the warm months. You will be hiking on a southwest-facing slope until you reach Holland Creek. It can be very hot during the afternoon of a summer day.

You do all of your climbing in the first 1.4 miles. This part of the trail is considered moderate. The remainder of the trail to Holland Creek is either flat or a gentle downhill. After you cross Holland Creek, you can continue your walk along the Holland-Gordon Trail and loop back to your car. The Holland- Gordon Trail is on a northwest-facing slope and shaded by the forest. This lovely trail passes through a forest characterized by lodgepole pine trees, spruces, larches, and Pacific yews. Mule deer, elk, and bears frequent the area. You can continue back to your vehicle after crossing Holland Creek at the outlet of Holland Lake. Turn right after you cross the bridge, and walk through the group camping area, the swimming beach area, and the two campgrounds.

Getting there
The trail is easily accessible. Turn on to Holland Lake Road, between mile markers 35 and 36, Highway 83. The road is distinguishable by a rustic sign directing you to Holland Lake Lodge. Follow the gravel road four miles, past the boat launch, campgrounds, and entrance to Holland Lake Lodge. The road terminates in a large parking area that can accommodate 20 vehicles.

Along the way

0.1 miles. Sign. East Holland Lake Connector Trail, #415.

0.9 miles. Begin ascent.

1.0 miles. Sign on spruce tree affirming trail #415.

1.1 miles. Junction with trail #192, East Foothills Trail.

1.2 miles. Junction with trail #42, Holland Creek Trail.

1.4 miles. Avalanche chute. The next 0.5 miles affords panoramic
      views of Holland Lake and the Mission Mountains Range.

1.7 miles. Panoramic view of Holland Creek.

2.2 miles. Cross Holland Creek on a footbridge.

2.3 miles. Junction with trail #35. Take the right turn toward Owl
      Packer Camp.

2.5 miles. Framed view of Holland Lake.

2.8 miles. Switchbacks.

4.0 miles. Glimpse Holland Lake Lodge across the lake.

4.5 miles. Owl Loop Road. Turn right toward Owl Creek Packer
      Camp.

5.0 miles. Bridge over Holland Creek. This is the outlet of Holland
      Lake.

6.3 miles. Parking area.

SWAN RIVER NATIONAL WILDLIFE REFUGE

Travel rating: Easy.
Distance: No maintained trail.
Walking time: Variable.
Trail use: Hiking and canoeing.
Elevation change: None.

Getting there
There are two ways to access the Swan River National Wildlife Refuge: turn west onto the refuge access road between mile markers 69 and 70 Highway 83, and by way of Porcupine Creek Road between mile markers 68 and 69. People choosing the Porcupine Creek Road access do so in order to float this section of the Swan River through the refuge.

The 1,567 acres Swan River National Wildlife Refuge contains marshland, forested river bottoms and meadows. The refuge supports at least 170 species of birds, many which find nesting habitat, including: bald eagles, great blue herons, and black terns. Canada geese, whistling swans, mallards and common goldeneyes winter in the open waters of the refuge.Depending on the season, you will find within the refuge, elk, deer, moose, bears, beaver, and river otters.

The refuge is closed to the public from March 1 to July 1 to protect nesting birds. The refuge is administered by the US Fish and Wildlife Sevice and was adopted by the Flathead Chapter of the National Audubon Society under their Adopt-A-Refuge program.

In 1986 The Nature Conservancy purchased nearly 400 acres of wetlands between the refuge and Porcupine Creek Road to the south. Known as the Swan River Oxbow Preserve, it was set aside to protect a rare aquatic plant known as Howellia aquatillis. The plant is known to grow in only four places on earth: two counties in Montana and two counties in Washington. The preserve has the world's largest single population of this endangered plant.

SALLY TOLLEFSON TRAIL

Travel rating: Easy.
Distance: 2 miles, round trip.
Walking time: 1 hour, round trip.
Trail use: Hiking.
Elevation change: None.

Getting there
Turn on to Porcupine Creek Road, between mile markers 68 and 69. Proceed 0.3 miles and turn right on the first available road. The parking area is 0.25 miles farther and can accommodate 12 vehicles.

This beautiful one-mile trail leads you to a wildlife viewing platform at an oxbow pond. A self-guided brochure is available at the trailhead. Expect damp trail conditions all summer.

This is an excellent trail to walk with children because there is an abundance of diversity for them to discover in a short easy hike.

Along the trail you will see Englemann's spruce trees, aspens, buckhorns, Douglas-firs, black cottonwoods, subalpine firs, Western white pines, alder, mushrooms, liverworts, lungworts, wildflowers, and white-tailed deer.

The Nature Conservancy has labeled several plant species with trailside signs.

MORRELL FALLS

Travel rating: Easy.
Distance: 4.6 miles, round trip.
Walking time: 2 hours, round trip.
Trail use: Moderate to heavy. Multiple users.
Elevation change: 145 feet gain.

Getting there
The trail is easily accessible. Turn onto Morrell Creek Road, at mile marker 15, Highway 83. The road is distinguished by Forest Service signs directing you to Morrell Falls. Follow the signs seven miles along the well-maintained road to a large parking area. The parking lot can accommodate 15 vehicles. There are toilet facilities at the trailhead. A drinking water source is not available. The trail is designated a National Recreational Trail. It receives heavy use during the warm months by hikers, horseback riders, and mountain bikers. The trail is relatively level and can be easily hiked by most family groups. Morrell Falls begins as a series of cascades that concludes with a waterfall.

The first half mile of the trail is distinguished by an even-aged stand of lodgepole pine. After leaving the lodgepole pine forest, you will enter a forest composed mostly of spruce and fir trees. Notice the varying height of the forest canopy (treetops), the direct sunlight reaching the forest floor, and the diversity of the undergrowth. This is in contrast to the lodgepole pine forest in which you have been walking. Which forest will sustain a greater diversity of plant and animal life?

As you near the falls, you will come across two small, shallow lakes. The first lake is more like a small pond. The rushing water you hear to your left is Morrell Creek. You will cross it on a footbridge. Shortly after crossing the bridge, you will follow the trail to your right along the base of a hill and next to the creek. Within the distance of a soccer field you will arrive at the base of the a double waterfall that crashes 90-feet to the valley floor. Both Morrell Creek and Morrell Falls are named for Fred Morrell, an early-day ranger in the Seeley Lake Ranger District.

Along the way
1.0 miles. Begin gentle ascent into a closed forest with lodgepole
         pines, spruce trees, and larches.
1.7 miles. First Morrell Lake.
1.8 miles. Shallow, 25-acre Morrell Lake.
2.1 miles. Footbridge over Morrell Creek.
2.3 miles. Morrell Falls.

Lodgepole Pine
The lodgepole pine tree gets its name from the fact that people traditionally have used the trunk of this tree to make the frames of their tepees (lodges). The tree is also frequently used to build the shells of log homes. The scientific name of this species does not describe the straight and long appearance of these trees. The botanists who first identified the characteristics of the lodgepole pine were studying specimens growing on the Pacific northcoast. There, the lodgepole growth pattern is affected by salt air and wind. This causes the lodgepole to grow twisted and stunted, hence the scientific name, Pinus contorta (contorted pine). The

common name given to these trees along the coast is the shorepine. It was several years later that botanists learned that the shorepine and the lodgepole are genetically the same. Nonetheless, the species retains the scientific name that describes it as a contorted tree.

GLACIER SLOUGH

Travel rating: Easy.
Distance: 2.6 miles, round trip.
Walking time: 1 hour, round trip.
Trail use: Light. Hiking and horseback riding.
Elevation change: 20 feet gain.

The Glacier Slough Trail is perfect for a hot afternoon or evening walk. Even during the heat of the day, the forest keeps the trail cool. Because the trail is mostly level, the walk to the slough can be accomplished by young and old, fit and not so fit. At the slough you will be rewarded with a beautiful vista of an area once a lake.

Getting there.
Turn on to Lindbergh Lake Road (USDA Forest Service Road 79) between mile markers 34 and 35, Highway 83. Travel three miles and follow the road toward Lindbergh Lake Campground, where the road forks. At 3.5 miles turn right at the sign directing you to "Trailhead" and "Bunyan Lake." Check your odometer and drive an additional 0.5 miles to the trail. The trailhead is at a tight left turn in the road and is marked with a small, rustic, obscure sign reading "Glacier Slough Trail No. 481."

Along the way
0.3 miles. Enter a small logged area.
0.6 miles. Large boulders on your left.
0.7 miles. Footbridge. Look for animal tracks in the mud.
0.8 miles. Small meadow. Listen for songbirds. Farther up the trail you will find an access road and a clear-cut.
1.3 miles. Glacier Slough.

This short trail will allow you to experience a young Douglas-fir, larch, and lodgepole pine forest. It will also allow you to see the effects of forestry practices as you pass through recent and not-so-recent, selectively logged and clear-cut lands.

Because of selective logging practices, the first 0.3 miles of the trail has some well-framed views of the Swan Range.

Notice the variation in temperature and humidity as you walk into and out of logged areas. One of the advantages of opening the forest through logging is to provide margins between deeper woods and open spaces. These margins encourage diversity in plant and animal life.

The Glacier Slough Trail is noted for abundant songbird life. The slough itself supports several species of waterfowl. The word slough brings to mind images of slow-moving muddy water. The water in Glacier Slough is crystal clear. The slough was at one time a lake along the Glacier Creek waterway. Topography and eutrophication have allowed the lake to fill with sediment and decaying plant life. The result is an area that is slowly changing to be a meadow, and eventually a forest. Glacier Creek will continue to course its way though the area.

Dippers

Regardless of the season you visit Glacier Slough, look for evidence of dippers on the rocks in Glacier Creek. Dippers are slate-gray fist-sized birds. Bird droppings on the boulders in the creek are a sign that dippers are in the area. They derive the common name of dipper from their characteristic bobbing mannerism. Dippers are known for making their nest out of mosses next to swiftly running water, often next to waterfalls. Dippers are fun to watch as they can actually walk on the stream bed as they feed on adult insects and insect larvae. Dippers will walk into the swiftly moving water and disappear. You will see them emerge a few feet away.

CLEARWATER LAKE

Travel rating: Easy.
Distance: 2.4 miles, round trip.
Walking time: 1 hour, round trip.
Trail use: Moderate use. Hiking.
Elevation change: 75 feet loss.

The lake is in heavily timbered country near the headwaters of the Clearwater River. It is about 125 acres and 40 feet deep. After leaving Clearwater Lake the water flows into a series of lakes, including: Rainy Lake, Lake Alva, Lake Inez, Seeley Lake, Salmon Lake, and the Elbow Lakes. The waters emptys into the Blackfoot River near Clearwater Junction (Montana Highways 200 and 83). At 35-miles in length, the river drains the southern portion of the 90-mile-long Seeley-Swan region.

Getting there
The Clearwater Loop Road (USDA Forest Service Road #4370) is between mile markers 28 and 29, Highway 83.
The trailhead is at seven miles on the well-maintained Forest Service road. The trailhead is adequately marked and usually easy to find because of the cars in the parking area.

There is parking for 10 vehicles. When you leave the trailhead for home, continue driving in a clockwise direction. The road loops back to Highway 83 and intersects the highway one mile south of Clearwater Loop Road.

Along the way
0.5 miles. Clearwater Lake.
2.0 miles. Outlet of Clearwater Lake. Look for beaver activity.
2.4 miles. Trail back to the parking area.

The walk to the lake is easy. Expect to meet hikers along the path and at the lake. At the lake you will have the option to continue on a two-mile loop around the lakeshore. A walk around the lake will afford you wonderful panoramic views of the lake, surrounding forest, and the peaks of the Swan Range in the Ptarmigan Mountain area.

The forest is predominantly lodgepole pine, Western larch, and Douglas-fir trees. Watch for the numerous waterfowl species that nest along the shore of the lake, including: buffleheads, goldeneyes, mallards, coots, and even loons. Listen for coyotes yelping in the evening.

Turquoise Lake

Holland Lake, at the outlet

Mission Mountains Range at Elk Creek

Swan River at Cold Creek Road

Oxbow Lake, Sally Tollefson Trail

Upper Cold Lake

Piper Lake

Crystal Lake

LAKE DINAH

Travel rating: Moderate.
Distance: 4 miles, round trip.
Walking time: 2 hours, round trip.
Trail use: Moderate. Hiking.
Elevation change: 140 feet gain.

Getting there

Turn west off Highway 83 on to Boy Scout Road, between mile markers 19 and 20. Travel 0.9 miles to Fawn Creek Road (U.S. Forest Service Road #4349). Turn right and proceed 4.1 miles. Turn right on the Lake Elsina Road (USDA Forest Service Road #465). Follow this road another 4.3 miles to an intersection that is signed for Lake Elsina. Turn left and travel approximately two miles to Lake Elsina. You will find the trailhead at the end of the road.

Wildflowers bloom later in the summer season around Lake Dinah. The beargrass display can be dramatic. This area supports white-tailed deer, moose, mountain lions, elk, Columbian ground squirrels, and bears.

Columbian Ground Squirrels

These colonial animals live throughout the Seeley-Swan. They are not gophers, but belong to the family of animals that includes marmots, flying squirrels, chipmunks, and prairie dogs. Plainsmen called them picket-pins, because their standing profile resembles the long, shepard's staff-like metal stake plainsmen used to "picket" their horses where trees were not available.

At 6,460 feet, the 36-acre Lake Dinah rests near the top of the Clearwater-Jocko Divide. Due to its altitude and its east-facing orientation, the basin receives a lot of snow. Indirect sunlight in the springtime means snow melts slowly. This cool alpine area is a great destination during a hot summer day at lower elevations. The lake is always cold and offers an exhilarating swimming opportunity at the right time of the season.

HOLLAND FALLS

Travel rating: Easy.
Distance: 3 miles, round trip.
Walking time: 90 minutes, round trip.
Trail use: Heavy. Hiking, snowshoeing, cross-country skiing.
Elevation change: 200 feet gain.

The trail to Holland Falls may be the most heavily used trail in the Swan Valley. You might encounter as many as 50 people, of all ages, sizes, and outdoor experience along the trail during the summer.

In wintertime, you will find outdoor enthusiasts on cross-country skis or snowshoes along the trail.Everyone will have Holland Falls as their quest.

It is no wonder that the trail receives heavy use. The spectacular waterfall and panoramic views of Holland Lake with the Mission Mountains Range as a backdrop are well worth the hike, ski, or snowshoe. The Holland Falls Trail is designated a National Recreational Trail.

Holland Creek has its headwaters in Upper Holland Lake. It tumbles four miles through a timbered canyon to Holland Lake. At 416 acres, Holland Lake is one of the largest bodies of water in the Swan Valley. After leaving Holland Lake, the creek runs an additional four miles until it empties into the Swan River at Pine Ridge Campground, just west of Highway 83.

Getting there

The trail is easily accessible. Turn on to Holland Lake Road, between mile markers 35 and 36, Highway 83. The road is distinguishable by a rustic sign directing you to Holland Lake Lodge. Follow the gravel road four miles, past the boat launch, campgrounds, and entrance to Holland Lake Lodge. At this point the road terminates in a large parking area that can accommodate 20 vehicles. This is a parking area for several trailheads. Not all the people using this parking area will be hiking to Holland Falls. Nonetheless, you will recognize this as one of the busiest trailheads along the Swan Front. The trailhead serves as the embarkation point for Holland Falls, Sapphire Lake, Necklace Lakes, Upper Holland Lake, and the Bob Marshall Wilderness. The first mile of the trail is a gentle walk along the north shore of Holland Lake and is rated as easy. The last third mile is steeper with broken rock outcroppings. This part of the trail is rated as moderate.

Along the way

0.2 miles. Trail junctions. Take Holland Falls Trail #416.
0.9 miles. Leave lake area. You begin your climb to the falls.
1.0 miles. Cross a bridge.
1.3 miles. Panoramic view of the Mission Mountains.
           The prominent mountain is McDonald Peak, located in
           the Mission Mountains Tribal Wilderness.
1.5 miles. Holland Falls.

The 50-foot waterfall, upper and lower lakes, and creek are named after Ben Holland. In 1897 he filed water rights on Holland Creek and for a homestead patent in 1904. While living in the valley, he prospected and worked as a ranger in the Upper Swan Valley. A note of caution: there is not an established viewpoint above or below Holland Falls. The jumble of rocks at the base of the falls can be treacherous, hiding sheer drop-offs. Be extra cautious with children.

INSPIRATION POINT

Travel rating: Moderate.
Distance: 10 miles, round trip.
Walking time: 6 hours round trip.
Trail use: Light. Hiking.
Elevation change: 300 feet gain.

The view from Inspiration Point is exhilarating. From here you are awarded with a commanding perspective of the middle of the Mission Mountains Range to the west.

Getting there.
Turn onto Goat Creek Road between mile markers 59 and 59. The access to Napa Point trailhead is well marked. However, the 12 mile road to the trailhead feels like a long trip in itself. The road is constructed like a typical mountain logging road, meaning it is narrow, rough, and steep with several tight switchbacks. The parking area at the trailhead can accommodate 10 vehicles.

Along the way.
2.2 miles. Junction with Soup Creek Trail.
2.5 miles. Trail junction to Inspiration Point. Follow right.
3.8 miles. Cross Swift Creek.
5.0 miles. Inspiration Point.

Native people from the Flathead Valley used several routes through the Swan Valley and over the Swan Range to access the buffalo country on the prairie. What is now known as the Napa Point Trail was in 1932 documented as a main passageway used by the Indians. The route follows Goat Creek over Inspiration Pass and exiting the mountains south of the town of East Glacier.

It is a good idea to get an early start on your walk to Inspiration Point. Most of your walk is in high alpine terrain along south and west-facing exposures. The trail receives harsh drying sunlight on clear summer afternoons.

The view at the trailhead is spectacular, as well it should be. After all, this is the site of the former Napa Point fire lookout. Most of the day hikes along the Swan Front require climbing before you reach alpine country. This trail does not. Most of your elevation gain along the Swan Front has been completed by reaching the trailhead.

The trail to Inspiration Point is a pathway through a subalpine fir forest of and lodgepole pines. In less than a half mile, the pathway leaves the forest and follows the ridgeline separating the Soup Creek drainage to the north and the Goat Creek drainage to the south. Across Goat Creek you will have views of the north-south Scout Creek Drainage and Bethal Creek drainage. Always looming ahead of you is the headwall of the Swan Front and your destination, Inspiration Point. The trail cuts east along the ridge, climbing moderately.

Along the ridge you will be treated to magnificant wildflower gardens of paintbrush, sego lilies, and glacier lilies. Hawks and falcons will use the thermal updrafts above the ridge to stay aloft while hunting. Closer to the ground are Clark's nutcrackers, pine siskins, nuthatches, song sparrows, chickadees, western tanagers, and northern flickers. Snow can stay into July at Inspiration Point. Large fields of glacier lilies, paintbrush, beargrass, and other alpine wildflowers grow in dense profusion near Inspiration Point.

Be aware of the prospects of thunderstorms. They build quickly and unexpectedly in this area. You will have little opportunity to find cover from a storm.

Pikas
The Seeley-Swan high country supports colonies of pikas, often referred to as rock rabbits. You will hear their short bugle-like warning squeaks when you come near their homes in the talus slopes. The size of a grapefruit, and with tiny ears, pikas live among the rocks and feed in the meadows on wildflowers and herbs. Picas do not hibernate but live under the snow eating the food that they "harvested" during the summer. Able to live but a few hours in temperatures above 77 degrees, global warming is threatening pika populations in Nevada, California, and Oregon.

PYRAMID LAKE

Travel rating: Strenuous.
Distance: 8 miles, round trip.
Walking time: 6 hours, round trip.
Trail use: Moderate. Hiking and horseback riding.
Elevation change: 1,640 feet gain.

Getting there
Turn onto Morrell Creek Road, at milemarker 15, Highway 83. Travel 1.1 miles to West Morrell Road #4353. Follow West Morrell Road six miles. Turn onto Pyramid Pass Road #4381, and travel 5.5 miles to the trailhead.

This is not an easy hike for your first of the season. The elevation gain is 1,640 feet in four miles. Some stretches of the trail exceed a grade of 8%. (A 7% grade is the limit of most mountain highways.) The Pyramid Pass Trail (Trail #416) is a popular entrance into the Bob Marshall Wilderness Area. You will be sharing the trail with outfitters and recreation horse parties. Yield to stock users. Stand on the downhill side and away from the trail. Horses can frighten easily in the back country.

The lower reaches of the trail are along abandoned logging access roads and through Trail Creek Valley. These areas of the trail afford spectacular views of the Seeley Lake area and the Mission Mountains Range. The upper portion of the trail crosses Trail Creek several times before arriving at a small unnamed lake. Pyramid Pass is a low saddle between wooded hills. The view to the east is into the drainage of the South Fork of the Flathead River. To the northwest is Pyramid Peak.

Pyramid Lake is another 0.25 miles beyond the 7,000-feet pass. Accessing the 10-acre lake is a downhill walk into the Bob Marshall Wilderness. Stay on trail #416, it is a well-used but unmarked trail heading north.

At 6,927 feet, Pyramid Lake is located in a stunning alpine setting just east of the imposing Pyramid Peak. There are no established trails to Pyramid Peak. Expect a difficult scramble if you try.

SMITH CREEK PASS

Travel rating: Strenuous.
Distance: 2 miles, round trip.
Walking time: 1 hour, round trip.
Trail use: Light. Hiking and horseback riding.
Elevation change: 3,740 feet gain.

Getting there.
Turn onto Falls Creek Road, USDA Forest Service Road #9551, be-tween mile markers 42 and 43, Highway 83. The Smith Creek Trail is often referred to as Trail #29. Follow the well-maintained gravel road three miles to a junction with Forest Service Road #9762. Turn right for an additional mile to the Smith Creek Trailhead.

The first mile of the trail offers a good example of the lower Swan Front ecosystem. The forest is dominated by old-growth stands of lodgepole pines, Western larch trees, and various species of fir trees. The understory is open, providing good viewing and sounds of Smith Creek to the south. The forest is cool and shaded, even on a hot summer afternoon. Expect snow to stay late in the spring-time along the protected areas of the trail.

At the one-mile mark, the trail makes a sharp turn to the north to climb into an old logged area. To the immediate right is access to Smith Creek. This is a good place to rest and enjoy the beauty of the creek before continuing.

The remainder of the hike to Smith Creek Pass is a steady climb up the ridge between Smith Creek and Condon Creek. Several times you will pass through logged areas that provide excellent views of the Swan Valley and Mission Mountains. The west-facing Swan Front receives intense sunlight. Clear-cut areas are hot during summer months. I recommend you start this hike by mid-morning. When not in the open, you will be walking through a cool forest with few vistas.

Smith Creek Pass is at 8,000 feet on a rocky ridgeline. Expect to find snow into early summer and late October at the pass. The view stretching out to the east is of the Little Salmon drainage in the Bob Marshall Wilderness.

THE JEWEL BASIN

Travel rating: Moderate.
Distance: 5 miles.
Walking time: 3 hours.
Trail use: Moderate. Hiking.
Elevation change: 825 feet gain.

The Jewel Basin is one of the foremost hiking areas in Montana. This exquisite 15,349-acre subalpine basin is sprinkled with 27 lakes of varying shapes and sizes, set within fairyland-like forests and surrounded by jagged shear cliffs. The profusion of wildflowers can be staggering, as hillsides, parks, and glades are painted in exquisite colors. Mid-July through August are the best times to witness the wildflower display. Along with the mountain peaks, wildflowers, lakes, and watercourses, the Jewel Basin has a great array of wildlife. From migratory to resident bird species, large mammals to the smallest vole, the Jewel Basin supports nearly every species of animal here at the time Montana became a state. There are several access points to the Jewel Basin and a 35-mile trail system within. This guide introduces you to one day hike that you can easily access from Highway 83.

Getting there
Turn off Highway 83 at Echo Lake Road, located between mile markers 88 and 89. Travel 2.5 miles to Noisy Creek Road, and turn right. After another seven miles of travel over the narrow gravel road, you will arrive at a large parking area.

This trail takes you on a loop overlooking the Twin Lakes, through lush subalpine meadows and back to the parking lot. Take Trail 8 from the trailhead and follow it northward two miles along the west-facing slope of the Swan Range. Dramatic views of the Upper Flathead Valley, Kalispell, and the Whitefish Range will appear. The trail eventually swings east and passes among dead trees, a scree field and through a knotch. You are now in the Jewel Basin. Turn right at the junction of Trail 7. Continue south on Trail 7 through meadows of wildflowers and subalpine forests and over small streams and rivulets to the junction of Trail 68. Follow Trail 68 to Trail 8. Trail 8 will take you back to the parking lot.

SIXMILE PEAK

Travel rating: Strenuous.
Distance: 11 miles, round trip.
Walking time: 7 hours, round trip.
Trail use: Moderate. Hiking and horseback riding.
Elevation change: 3,400 feet gain.

Getting there.
Turn on to Sixmile Road on the east side of Highway 83 between mile markers 72 and 73. The trailhead is located 4 miles from here.

The Sixmile Trail to Six Mile Peak is recommended for hikers who are experienced with rigorously difficult mountain trails. The view from the old lookout site on Sixmile Peak is the attaction for most hikers. At four miles the trail intersects Alpine Trail #7. Sixmile Trail leads west and is infreqently maintained. In places it may appear as a game trail. I advise a topographic map

HALL LAKE

Travel rating: Easy to Strenuous.
Distance: 10 miles, round trip.
Walking time: 6 hours, round trip.
Trail use: Light. Hiking and horseback riding.
Elevation change: 2,065 feet gain.

Getting there
Turn east from Highway 83 at the Laughing Horse Lodge between mile markers 71 and 72. Follow this road about three-quarters of a mile past a guest ranch. The trailhead is at a large parking area.

Most day-hikers will find the lower two miles of the Hall Lake Trail suitable enough for a leasurely excursion. This part of the trail is rated as easy. There are many species of wildflowers and songbirds that inhabit the forest environment before the trail crosses Groom Creek. After crossing the creek the trail begins a long three mile, 3,000 feet vertical climb to wonderful views and Hall Lake. The lake is to the northwest of Hall Peak in a subalpine setting surrounded by talus and brush. It is a deep 12-acre lake high above the community of Swan Lake.

SAPPHIRE LAKE AND
UPPER HOLLAND LAKE

Travel rating: Strenuous.
Distance: 14 miles, loop.
Walking time: 7 to 8 hours.
Trail use: Moderate. Hiking and horseback riding.
Elevation change: 2,970 feet gain to Sapphire Lake,
*   then a 855 feet drop to Upper Holland Lake.*

Getting there.
Turn onto Holland Lake Road, between mile markers 35 and 36,
Highway 83. Follow the gravel road four miles, past the boat
launch, campgrounds, and entrance to Holland Lake Lodge. The
road terminates in a large parking area that can accommodate
twenty vehicles. This is a parking area for several trailheads.
The trailhead serves as the embarkation point for Holland Falls,
Sapphire Lake, Necklace Lakes, Upper Holland Lake, and the Bob
Marshall Wilderness.

Along the way.
0.2 miles. Trail junctions. Take East Holland Lake Trail #415.
1.0 miles. Trail junction with East Foothills Trail #192. Stay on
Trail #415.
1.5 miles. Trail junction with Holland Lookout Trail #42. Take this
trail.
3.5 miles. Holland Lookout Pass.
4.0 miles. Junction with Trail #110. Turn right.
7.5 miles. Upper Holland Lake. Pick up the Holland Gordon Trail
#35 to descend to the valley floor along Holland Creek.
12.9 miles. Junction with Trail #192, East Foothills Trail.
13.0 miles. Follow East Holland Lake Connector Trail, #415.
14.0 miles. Parking lot.

The trails to and from Sapphire Lake and Upper Holland Lake
can be joined together in order to make a loop for a long day
hike. Hiking the trail as a loop will take you near the site of the
Holland Lookout, by Sapphire Lake, by Upper Holland Lake, and
along Holland Creek.

Sapphire Lake is a 15-acre high alpine lake located in a rocky basin. The lake is at the western edge of Waldbillig Mountain and is just 1.5 miles west of Upper Holland Lake. Sapphire Lake is west of the Bob Marshall Wilderness Area.

Sapphire Lake

Upper Holland Lake is also outside the Bob Marshall Wilderness below the western crest of the Swan Range. The lake is about 50 acres, in subalpine country. The Holland Gordon Trail #35 is the most heavily used in the Swan Lake Ranger District. It provides common access to the Bob Marshall Wilderness Area from the Swan Valley floor. This portion of the Holland Gordon Trail follows Holland Creek as it flows four miles from Upper Holland Lake to Holland Lake. Along the way you will encounter numerous unnamed waterfalls, cascades, and sparkling cold, azure pools.

Red Squirrels
The red squirrel species inhabits the forests of the Seeley- Swan. This smallest of all tree squirrels is locally known as the pine squirrel. These tree acrobats delight hikers with their endearing antics. You can detect pine squirrels by sight or sound. Their noisy chattering is a territorial cry. With populations of two squirrels to three acres, their territories overlap. Red squirrels do not hibernate, and can live 10 years if they elude owls, martens, foxes, and bobcats.

BOND LAKE

Travel rating: Strenuous.
Distance: 14 miles, round trip.
Walking time: 8 hours, round trip.
Trail use: Moderate. Hiking and horseback riding.
Elevation change: 2,500 feet gain.

Getting there
The trailhead is located on the east side of Highway 83 at mile marker 70. Do not park on the access road. There is a small parking lot at the trailhead.

Along the way
1.5 miles. Trail crosses Bond Creek on a footbridge.
2.0 miles. Trail encounters a series of waterfalls and begins its ascent to the Bond Lake Basin.
5.0 miles. Bond Lake Basin.

Bond Creek Trail leads to Bond Lake, located high on the Swan Range front. The first two miles are swampy in spots and follow the creek. It is relatively easy walking most of the summer. At other times it is difficult due to dense undergrowth encroaching on the trail. An early morning hike can soak clothing as it rubs against the foliage. At two miles you arrive at a series of waterfalls. Some are near the trail and others about 25 yards off the main trail. One waterfall drops 50 feet. Goats frequent this area. Past the waterfall the trail moves out of the riparian habitat and begins a long climb into high country. The trail becomes very steep in parts exceeding a grade of 25%. Close to Bond Lake the trail goes through a steep timbered canyon. Dense annual undergrowth encroaches on the trail as you approach the Bond Lake Basin.

Bond Lake is deep, sitting in a timbered cirque on the north slope of Spring Slide Mountain. The lake is about five acres and makes for a good place to rest before returning to the trailhead or hiking another mile to higher country and Trinkus Lake. Dense growth of annual plants encroach the trail to Trinkus Lake. Beyond Trinkus Lake, another 0.25 miles is the junction of Bond Creek Trail and Alpine Trail #7 with access to Jewel Basin.

JIM GIRARD MEMORIAL GROVE

Travel rating: Easy.
Distance: No established trail.
Walking time: Does not apply.
Trail use: Hiking.
Elevation change: None.

Getting there
Turn west on Boy Scout Road, mile marker 14, Highway 83.
Travel approximately two miles and cross a bridge over the
Clearwater River at the outlet of Seeley Lake. Pass the sign for
Camp Paxson.

The entrance to the Jim Girard Memorial Tamaracks Grove is about 100 yards farther on the left hand side of Boy Scout Road. The area is closed to vehicle travel December 1 to May 15.

The Jim Girard Memorial Tamaracks Grove is more an area for free-flowing discovery than a hiking area.

As you wander through the grove you will see evidence of early logging in the Seeley area, as well as the trees that missed being cut. Some of the trees are over 600 years old. Your companions in the grove might include, moose, elk, bears, bald eagles, ospreys or coyotes.

CLEARWATER RIVER CANOE TRAIL

Travel rating: Easy.
Distance: Canoeing 3.5 miles, hiking 1.5 miles.
Walking time: 4 hours, round trip.
Trail use: Hiking and canoeing.
Elevation change: 7 feet loss.

The Clearwater River Canoe Trail is a unique experience in the Seeley-Swan Area. It combines a canoe trip along the Clearwater River before the river empties into Seeley Lake. Once you reach the head of the lake, you paddle across to the Seeley Lake Ranger Station. You then access your vehicle after a 1.5-mile hike back to the parking lot. The combined experience of floating the river and walking the shoreline will give you the chance to observe the fauna and flora from both perspectives.

Getting there

The access to the Clearwater River Canoe Trail is located between mile markers 18 and 19, Highway 83. Turn on to USDA Forest Service Road #17597 and travel 0.7 miles to the trailhead. There is parking available for 14 vehicles.

It requires two hours to float the 3.5 miles of the Clearwater River as it meanders in this low-lying valley. There is no white water, but you will experience a constant flow at about two miles an hour.

Early morning is the best time to do the float trip and observe the myriad resident and migrating waterfowl. You may expect to see the following birds along the route: common loons, bald eagles, ospreys, kingfishers, American bitterns, great blue herons, goldeneyes, American coots, various woodpeckers, and swallows. Stop at the Seeley Lake Ranger Station north of the town of Seeley Lake to acquire a copy of Birds of Seeley Lake. This is a checklist of seasonal, common, and rare birds found in the area.

The Clearwater River also attracts numerous wildlife species. You may see white-tailed deer, moose, mink, muskrats, beaver, elk, otters, and bears on your float trip or your return to your car.

HOLLAND LAKE NATURE TRAIL

Travel rating: Easy.
Distance: 1 mile loop.
Walking time: 40 minutes.
Trail use: Light. Hiking and cross-country skiing.
Elevation change: None.

The Holland Lake Nature Trail provides a leisurely hike through the environment of the Holland Creek drainage. The trail loops through the forest north of Holland Lake. You can obtain an interpretive pamphlet at the trailhead. The pamphlet introduces you to the natural and cultural history of the Holland Lake area.

Getting there

Turn onto Holland Lake Road between mile markers 35 and 36, Highway 83. Travel four miles on the well-maintained Forest Service road past the junction of Owl Creek Road. You will find a boat ramp and group campground on your right. Past the group campground will be a sign directing you to a swimming beach. Park in the swimming beach parking lot. The Holland Lake Nature Trail begins on the opposite side of the gravel road.

CLEARWATER GAME RANGE

Travel rating: Easy.
Distance: No maintained trail.
Walking time: Variable.
Trail use: Automobile, mountain biking and hiking.
Elevation change: None.

Getting there

Turn into the parking area on the east side of Highway 83 at mile marker 3. This is the western entrance to the game range.
The 65,000 acre Clearwater Game Range is open between May 15 through mid-November. There are no established trails. Walking the dirt road may put you near elk, mule deer, whitetailed- deer, coyotes, bears, lots of waterfowl, and songbirds. Hawks, owls and woodpeckers are abundant within the range.

SWAN RIVER
NATURE TRAIL

> *Travel rating: Easy.*
> *Distance: 2 miles, round trip.*
> *Walking time: 1 hour, round trip.*
> *Trail use: Moderate. Multiple use, no motorized.*
> *Elevation change: None.*

Getting there

This is the only trail described in this guide that is not accessed by way of Montana Highway 83. The trail begins at the eastern termination of Grand Avenue in downtown Big Fork. You might find it better to park in downtown Big Fork and walk the short distance to the trailhead rather than try to secure a parking place at the limited space available at the beginning of the trail.

The trail follows the north bank of the Swan River along an abandoned roadbed that was the original road from Big Fork leading east. The road was abandoned in the 1950s in favor of Highway 209 to the south of the Swan River. The old roadbed was converted to a nature trail that was officially established in 1995.

The Swan River Nature Trail provides a leisurely walk along the last two miles of the Swan River before it empties into Big Fork Bay and Flathead Lake. The trail is privately owned by Art Whitney and PacificCorp. Volunteers in the Big Fork community have raised money for maintenance and improvements. The entire length of the trail is flat and wide. This allows multiple-use interests to coexist. You may encounter hikers, joggers, bicyclists, and equestrians along the trail. You should also expect to find numerous species of wildflowers and songbirds inhabiting the area.

The section of Swan River that the nature trail follows is considered world-class whitewater. The last mile before entering Big Fork Bay approaches class IV status. During late May hundreds of spectators come to the Swan River Nature Trail to watch "The Wild Mile" kayak competion. More than 200 participants from around the world often compete for recognition.

GOAT CREEK
WATCHABLE WILDLIFE TRAIL

Travel rating: Easy.
Distance: 1 mile, round trip.
Walking time: 1 hour, round trip.
Trail use: Hiking.
Elevation change: None.

Getting there

Take Goat Creek Road (USDA Forest Service Road #554), between mile markers 58 and 59, for 1.5 miles, then turn right onto Squeezer Creek Road.

You will find the trail after traveling about two miles on this road. There is parking for at least six vehicles.

The Goat Creek Watchable Wildlife Area is an explosion of sights and sounds on a spring morning. You may see and hear the following birds to add to your "life list": red-eyed vireo, Western tanager, Swainson's thrush, brown creeper, Northern flicker, ruby-crowned kinglet, chipping sparrow, song sparrow, hairy woodpecker, Audubon's warbler, and pileated woodpecker.

Cited in Steve Lamar's Swan Valley Place Names, (2008), longtime resident Leonard Moore declared that Squeezer got its name from a squatter forced (squeezed) off land in this area during homesteading days.

SPRUNGER-WHITNEY NATURE TRAIL

Travel rating: Easy.
Distance: 2 miles, round trip.
Walking time: 1 hour, round trip.
Trail use: Hiking.
Elevation change: 30 feet gain.

Getting there
The trail is easily accessible. Turn onto the Point Pleasant Camp-ground road between mile markers 63 and 64, Highway 83. Turn right at the first opportunity. The trailhead is at the parking lot.

This nature trail follows the old Swan Highway for approximately one mile. The roadbed is believed to be constructed over a trail historically used by the Pend d'Oreille (pronounced ponder-ay) and Salish peoples. The route from the Flathead Valley through the Swan Valley is thousands of years old.

This area of the Swan Valley was a favorite place to hunt, fish, and gather berries. The forest is interspersed with multi-aged trees. Ancient Western larch trees are prominent in the forest. The Western larch is one of only three tree species that are cone bearing (coniferous) and deciduous (dropping their needles each autumn).

Note the tiny needles that litter the forest floor. Can you name the other two tree species that are deciduous and coniferous? The other two coniferous deciduous-trees are the dawn redwood, native of northern China, and the bald cypress, native to the southeastern United States.

The Sprunger-Whitney Nature Trail was built and maintained by the Friends of the Wild Swan, a nonprofit advocacy group located in Swan Lake.

EVERCHANGING FOREST TRAIL

Travel rating: Easy.
Distance: 1.2 miles, partial loop.
Walking time: 1 hour.
Trail use: Hiking.
Elevation change: None.

Getting there

The Everchanging Forest Trail is located at the Swan Ecosystem Center, between mile markers 42 and 43, Highway 83. Turn at the USDA Forest Service Condon Work Center, and park at the Swan Ecosystem Center building. The parking lot is large and can accommodate several cars. Signs will direct you to the trailhead from the parking lot.

A visit to the Swan Ecosystem Center is a must if you arrive during regular business hours. The center is easy to find and houses an information desk, nature center, handicapped-accessible restrooms, and office space. The center is a good place to inquire about local conditions, get an introduction to the natural and cultural history of the Upper Swan Valley, and pick up a copy of the Everchanging Forest Trail self-guided brochure. You can also get a copy of the brochure at the trailhead if you arrive outside of normal business hours.

The purpose of the Everchanging Forest Trail is to provide an appreciation of "some of the forces of change at work in Upper Swan Valley forests," and to help you learn about "some of the plants and animals that depend on these forests." The design of the trail accomplishes these goals by leading you through three areas: a closed-canopy environment, an open ponderosa pine forest, and a streamside forest. Along the way, you will encounter displays and exhibits that will help you appreciate the forest environment of the Upper Swan Valley.

The Everchanging Forest Trail is a cooperative effort sponsored by the Swan Ecosystem Center, Swan Lake Ranger District, Flathead National Forest, Missoula County Department of Natural Resources and Conservation, and the National Forest Foundation.

BIG LARCH NATURE TRAIL

Travel rating: Easy.
Distance: 0.5 miles, loop.
Walking time: 1 hour.
Trail use: Hiking.
Elevation change: None.

Getting there
Turn west off Highway 83 between mile markers 14 and 15 on the access road to the Big Larch Campground. Take the first right turn after entering the campground. The road ends in a parking lot with a sign welcoming you to the Big Larch Nature Trail.

A brochure, available at the trailhead, invites you to explore the natural history of this riparian and forested area. You will encounter rotting logs, lichen-covered trees, birds, and wildflowers. If you are lucky you will see signs of a red fox, like the one pictured above.